Addicted to Average

RICCARDO L. HARRIS

PUBLISHER
Motivation Squared

ADDICTED TO AVERAGE

Motivation Squared

Publishing History:
Hard cover edition published July 2022 by Motivation Squared
944 S. Topeka - Wichita, Kansas 67211

Cover Design by Riccardo Harris
Pictures by:
Gaberial Booker

https://www.gaberialbookcreativevisuals.com

An application to register this book for cataloging has been submitted to the Library of Congress.
ISBN 978-1-7360597-9-1
Printed in the United States of America
2 3 4 5 6 7 8 9 10

There is no passion to found playing small in settling for a life that is less than the one you are capable of living.

Nelson Mandela

Foreword

Michealangelo's statue of "David," considered the only depiction of David in the moment before he killed Goliath, poses a profound question: "Do I dare?"

David likely thought, standing there with his sling and stone, if I throw this stone and miss, I'm one dead Israelite. It if throw it and only wound him, I'm in the same situation. But if I defeat him, I'll have done something great for myself and for my people.

We all find ourselves in fleeting but potentially fortuitous moments where we ask ourselves, "do I dare?" Most of us shrink from the moment. We retreat into safe but unproductive comfort. We blink.

Pastor and author Riccardo Harris shares in his thoughtful new book, "Addicted to Average," that God calls us to venture beyond comfort and safety to claim the greatness He placed inside us.

Riccardo offers readers a path forward, sharing his own painful trials and joyous triumphs, and how despite material success, he'd found, like so many of us, he was not answering God's inscription of greatness on his heart.

His book is a spiritual GPS, helping us navigate a fundamental tenet of Christianity: daring to step out on faith, daring to claim what's rightfully ours, daring to be all God wants us to be.

Mark McCormick
New York Times Best Selling Author

Contents

Introduction

I woke up in the middle of the night and I couldn't go back to sleep. I turned on the television and began to flip through the channels hoping to find something I could watch and possibly fall back to sleep while watching. While skimming through the channels, I came across the old 90's movie, New Jack City. The movie highlights the drug epidemic and how crack cocaine ravaged urban neighborhoods. Nino Brown, the proverbial big-time drug dealer, builds his kingdom while the police attempt to bring him down. In the midst of all of the drama we are introduced to a character named Benny "Pookie" Robinson, who is addicted to crack cocaine. His character was played by Chris Rock. Pookie's recovery and his agreement to go undercover to help to bring down Nino Brown's empire ultimately leads to his death.

I've seen this movie many times, but each time I watch it, I see something new and different. This night the message came through Pookie's life. Pookie had an addiction to crack cocaine. His character fits the image of a crack addicted individual. He is unkempt, unclean, his hair is not combed, his teeth are rotten, and he is hustling, trying to make enough money for that next hit. There is a scene where Ice T's character (Detective Scotty Appleton) finds Pookie in a crack house. Pookie is being abusive to a woman who he had been smoking with. Detective Scotty grabs him to stop him from abusing the lady. He pulls him away from her. Pookie recognizes him as a cop and calls it out. Words are exchanged and Detective Scotty holds a gun to his face holds and says, "shut up. I should blow your brains out." Pookie's response was profound. He tries to explain about beating on the girl. He said, "Don't hurt me man. This crack shit has got me. I don't have no control over it. I tried to kick it, but, the shit just be calling me man, be calling me man. I just gotta go to it. I need help man." The very thing that he was addicted to was calling him.

We all have our own vices or addictions, things that affect us and disrupts our path and our purpose. Whether it's alcohol, drugs, sex, or gambling, we can become addicted to it. What may have started out as fun or a way to temporarily escape from the current reality, the use of drugs or alcohol and the like, has impacted many lives. Some people are workaholics, lie-aholics, drama-aholics and like Pookie said, it calls us and we gotta go to it.

As I was watching New Jack City the Spirit of the Lord spoke to me about addictions. He told me, "You are addicted to something as well." I searched my behavior and reasoned and responded, I don't drink, I don't smoke, I don't do anything in excess. Then the most chilling words I'd ever heard the Lord speak to me hit my spirit. The Spirit said, *"You are addicted to average!"* The words cut me deeply. I couldn't even enjoy the rest of the movie and I knew that I wasn't going back to sleep. I must admit, I kept hearing those words reverberating in my spirit over and over again…*Addicted to Average, Addicted to Average, Addicted to Average!*

I was offended by those words. I took offence because as I looked back over my life, I felt like I had accomplished some great things. I've been married for 30 years, I am the father of three beautiful children, and the grandfather of five grandchildren. I have been a minister for 29 years and a pastor for 27 years. I purchased my own home at the age of 25 and I am an executive on my job. Basically, I was giving God my resume or my CV.

God is not impressed with our resumes. He is not moved by our accomplishments. I thought by telling him of all of my accomplishments I could convince Him that I was not 'addicted to average'. It is easy to get caught up with all of the things we have done, the odds we've overcome and the victories we've won, but like I said, God is not impressed with our accomplishments. When God speaks to us and gives a revelation there has to be some truth to it. How am I addicted to average? I asked. To get further insight I looked up the words addicted and average in the dictionary.

Addicted

strongly inclined to do, use, or indulge in something repeatedly "Addicted." Merriam-Webster.com Dictionary, Merriam-Webster, https://www.merriam-webster.com/dictionary/addicted.

Average

The Merriam Webster Dictionary has a few definitions for the word average. The definition that resonates with me and my life is: **not out of the ordinary: COMMON.**

--Addicted to average means I am addicted to comparing myself to other people. It also says I'm okay with where I am. I am okay with playing it safe. Instead of being addicted to average, I'd say I am risk averse. I don't want to mess up or do anything that's considered radical. I stay in my comfort zone.

Average is a mindset

Some people may be offended by the term average. It is a term that describes not great news, not poor, but in between. Some may say I strive for greatness, but I accept what I get. This thinking minimizes your capacity. It also minimizes the things that you can and cannot accomplish. For me, this means I accept whatever comes to me. There is no trying, there is just accepting. Whatever happens, happens. When we measure our worth, value or success based upon the tasks we have completed, we are missing something. Checking a box is not the only indicator of success. Doing what we were created to do contributes to that success. Living life to the fullest should be the ultimate goal. God's plan.

My addiction to average has kept me in a comfort zone for many years. I have been satisfied with where I am. I've settled and missed out on greatness because I had experienced a moderate level of success. Instead of comparing myself to others and their accomplishments, I have to know what God has placed inside of me (purpose). I am being measured on the fulfillment of my capacity and how I am reaching that capacity. It is internal, not external. I know when I am giving my best, my all, 100 percent. I also know when I am skating by and doing the bare minimum. Although the bare minimum that I do has an effect, by doing that I am cheating myself and others from experiencing the greatness inside of me. I am also doing God a disservice.

Chapter One

Purpose

[9] A man's heart plans his way, But the Lord directs his steps.

Proverbs 16:9 (NKJV)

The late great Dr. Myles Munroe was an expert on teaching about purpose. He said, "*The greatest tragedy in life is not death, but life without a reason. It is dangerous to be alive and not know why you were given life.*"

I talk to people often who say, "I don't know what I'm supposed to be doing." The message, I don't know my purpose. When we don't know our purpose, it is easy to settle for anything that comes our way. The real measure of greatness should be based upon the fulfilment of our capacity. Our greatness is usually measured by someone on the outside looking in seeing what we are doing. Our value is judged by what they perceive, but greatness is something between you and God. It is the purpose that he has given you. Your purpose does not look like the purpose anyone else has. Your purpose looks like what God has in store for you; what He created for you to do, achieve, to accomplish.

God told Jeremiah, *"before I formed you in your mother's womb I knew you"* (Jeremiah 1:5). God is letting us know that he knows who we are and he knows what we're supposed to be doing, and sometimes that is difficult for us to grasp. It is difficult for us to understand because we can't see the plan...He (God)has the plan. This is faith. We should function by faith.

> ***For I know the plans I have for you," declares the LORD, "plans to prosper you and not to harm you, plans to give you hope and a future.***
>
> ***Jeremiah 29:11 NIV***

I flew on an airplane for the first time when I was 14 years old. A few people from my junior high school traveled to Europe during the summer of 1984. What a way to begin flying. I saw the great historical places like the Eiffel Tower in Paris, the Colosseum in Rome, the Vatican, the Sistine chapel, and the great canals of Venice. I didn't realize the greatness of that trip until later in life. Now, almost 40 years later I appreciate the lessons that I learned.

As I got older, traveling by plane was not something I did regularly. About 10 years ago I took a new job that would require me to travel frequently by plane. Flying on an airplane stressed me out. During the entire flight, every bump or turbulence the plane experienced made me anxious. In the beginning I was terrified. I remember traveling to some destinations and not enjoying my time there because I was worried about the return flight. In time I learned to love flying. It took a little while but the fear left.

Before each flight, one of the flight attendants gives the safety protocol speech about fastening your seatbelt and other emergency procedures. An oxygen mask is in the description. They say, if the cabin loses pressure, an oxygen mask will fall down from the ceiling. These instructions describe how to put on an oxygen mask, and it is followed by the next statement:

Put on your own mask first, **before YOU HELP** *others."*

My professional life has been multifaceted. I am an educator and a pastor. I have helped young people who experienced abuse or neglect, suffered from emotional disturbances. I served as a high school teacher and a coach. I've spent over 30 years helping people. All of my jobs have involved helping people. I am a helper. I want others to be successful. I've poured out my soul, sacrificed my wants and needs to help others. This is noble but I have neglected myself.

The instructions from the flight attendant teaches everyone a valuable lesson, and that is a lesson of self-care. If you don't take care of yourself, you cannot adequately help anyone else. What have I been doing? What about me? Helping young people or adults, is serious to me. As long as I am helping someone else, I cannot focus on my purpose and accomplishing the things set for me. I'm also ignoring the things that weigh me down. I've been so busy helping others with their oxygen masks that I cannot breathe.

The Apostle Paul says something profound in his first letter to the Corinthians. He says,

> ***"Everyone who competes in the games goes into strict training. They do it to get a crown that will not last, but we do it to get a crown that will last forever. Therefore, I do not run like someone running aimlessly; I do not fight like a boxer beating the air. No, I strike a blow to my body and make it my slave so that after I have preached to others, I myself will not be disqualified for the prize."***
>
> ***1 Corinthians 9:25-27 NIV***

Paul is speaking about helping other people and forgetting about himself. I've done this so many times that it has become natural to me. I have to make it a priority to put on my oxygen mask first, before I try to help someone else. To the helper, this will be challenging. I'm not being myself if I'm not helping someone, some may say. This is neglecting yourself or even martyrdom, a willingness to die for what you believe in. The truth is, nobody is killing me, I am killing myself. I'm doing this by ignoring the traumatic things that I have experienced in my life. Shake it off. Keep going. Those are the things I have always said to myself, but I was hurting on the inside.

I know that God created me to help other people. To be the best me that I can be, I have to be healthy and heal. We are all created differently. No two people are the same. Everyone's purpose is unique. Keeping myself busy with helping others distracted me from facing my issues.

Paul also said in his letter to the Corinthians,

> ***"I've become all things to all people that I may win some." 1 Corinthians 9:22***

The need to be needed

Wanting to belong, trying to fit in and not stand out, and/or operating below the best you that you can be., contributes to settling for average. Brene' Brown says in her book, Braving the Wilderness, "*True belonging is the spiritual practice of believing in and belonging to yourself so deeply that you can share your most authentic self with the world and find sacredness in both being a part of something and* standing *alone in the wilderness. True belonging doesn't require you to change who you are; it requires you to be who you are."*

Operating completely within your purpose requires authenticity and vulnerability.

Chapter Two

What's in Your Bag?

I carry a backpack wherever I go. One day I was at work and I was getting ready to leave my office and head to an appointment. I asked someone, hey will you hand me my backpack? I needed it for my next meeting. She grabbed the backpack and as she picked it up she said, Whoa! What's in your backpack? Why is it so heavy?

I started laughing a little bit but I started thinking to myself. What are the things that I carry in my bag? I have a laptop computer. I have another laptop computer. I have some files. I have some notebooks. I have some pens. I have all of these different things that I believe I may need. I keep all of the items in there just in case.

What things do you have in your bag? What are you're taking with you from place to place to place, from situation to situation? We do that in life. We carry things in our mind and subconscious. We take them with us. Past relationships, past experiences, successes and failures, those things shape and mold us into being who we are today.

I don't need all of the things in my bag. I know I don't, but I have them in there just in case. The extra things that I carry hinders my walk. It slows me down. That's true with the things that we carry in life too. Those are the things that slows us down. We hold on to it, whether it's a heartbreak, or a situation where somebody didn't treat us the right way. We carry that, we take that with us.

The Word of god tells us in Hebrews 12:1, "*to lay aside every weight and the sin that so easily besets us, and let us run with patience the race that is set before us.*

Sometimes it is difficult to let go of things. We hold on to our hurt, our pain, our disappointments. We are hoarders of our letdowns. We pitch our tent and stay there. If we put our trust in God, we can learn how to let things go. It isn't easy, but with God all things are possible.

Things weigh us down and God wants us to be willing to set them aside. I know that it's difficult to do. It's difficult but how do I lay aside those things that have hurt me so badly? How do I lay aside those things that injured me? How do I set them down? That is where your relationship with God comes in. You have to trust God enough to say, God I believe that you're bigger than my hurt.

I believe you're bigger than my pain. I believe you're bigger than my sorrow. Please take this away from me now.

It's hard for us and I know it's tough because we have allowed those situations to define us. They have defined our lives, they have defined our walk and we use those things to explain why we act a certain way or how we treat people. If we are willing to look in our bag and begin to assess what things we need and what things can we lay aside, we can begin to grow. What are you carrying that you cannot leave behind?

I was carrying some things that prevented me going to the next level. There may be some things that you carry that is preventing you from your breakthrough. What is blocking you from experiencing the greatness that God has for you? You can't get it and you can't see it because you're holding on to these things. If you're willing to let go, if you will say God, I need help with this, your life will be much better.

Trauma

According to the American Psychological Association, trauma is defined as, *"an emotional response to a terrible event like an accident, rape or natural disaster."*

I've experienced some traumatic things in my life. Those traumatic experiences have arrested my development in some ways. Many people experience some type trauma in their lives, from physical abuse to sexual abuse to verbal abuse, neglect, heartbreak or rejection. The list goes on and on. The pain is carried deep within.

How does trauma impact a person's life? I read an amazing book by Bessel Van Der Kolk, M.D. called, The Body Keeps Score: Brain, Mind and Body in the Healing of Trauma. This book explains some of what our body goes through when we experience a traumatic event. It says, "Trauma compromises the area of the brain that communicates the physical embodied feeling of being alive."

Life as we know it is affected by trauma. How we think, reason and process things is impacted. Trauma looks different for all of us. Everyone has experienced trauma in their lives and everyone doesn't respond in the same way. I never called it trauma. I didn't know that some of the trauma that I have experienced in my lifetime has affected the person that I am today. I have fears and attitudes about certain things. Some of it is based upon the things I've gone through or what I have seen. I pride myself on being an overcomer. I have overcome a lot of hurt and pain. I shake it off and keep moving. Shaking it off was a false front. I was tucking or hiding my pain to keep from dealing with it. Healing from traumatic events can be challenging.

I shared earlier about my first trip on an airplane when I was 14 years old. Something happened to me on that trip that I have kept hidden for 38 years. Our hotel in Paris was the Hotel Est. We were there for a few days. We wanted to tour the Louvre Museum, but when we arrived we learned that the staff members were on strike, so the museum was closed. One day we were standing outside our hotel and my friend and I were approached by some men. They were talking to us and I felt like it was inappropriate, so we went back to our room.

Three of us shared a room together (Me, Tre' and Skip). All of the windows in the room faced a courtyard. We looked out of the window and we saw the guys that we saw outside of the hotel. They were talking to us and I lost it. I said some choice words telling them to leave us alone. A few floors below the guys that were talking to us, there were some other guys looking out of their window. They started cursing at us in another language and pointing at us. A few minutes later there was a knock on the door. Then there was banging on the door. We placed one of the beds against the door and Skip sat on the bed. The banging on the door continued. I was terrified. Eventually the door was broken down. I could see the door coming off the hinges. The people banging on the door entered our room. They walked past Skip and Tre' and they came towards me. One of the men picked me up and tossed me across the room toward the door. I wasn't hurt, but I was scared. They picked me up again and threw me outside of the room. This time I landed near the stairs. I knew that I would be hurt or even killed if I was thrown down the stairs, so I jumped up and ran down the stairs as fast as I could. I made it to the first floor. I started banging on room doors hoping someone would let me in. I am thankful that someone opened the door. The guys in who opened the door were part of our tour group. I was crying and trying to explain what happened. That night, I slept under the bed in that room.

Mr. Anderson, our sponsor, was told what happened to me, so he started investigating. He found out that the group that broke into our room was part of the Yugoslavian national soccer team. They had lost a game in the European tournament and they were on edge. They believed I was insulting them by yelling out of the window. They did not know that I wasn't talking to them, I was talking to someone else. The next day, we were walking through the streets of Paris and we saw the people from the soccer team. One of the men pointed in our direction and started running toward me. I ran as fast as I could. I found an entrance to the subway, so I ran down there. I waited a little while before coming back to the street. By then, they were gone.

For most of my life I hid this. I didn't tell anyone. This was traumatic for me. I was 14 years old in foreign country all alone. I have nightmares from time to time and most of the time I am running from something or someone. This trauma, even though I hid it, was haunting me. Trauma will keep you bound. I have experienced a few traumatic events during my life, some have been minor and some have been extreme. Trauma affects our growth and our progress. It manifests in different ways. One way it manifests is by fear. Being afraid of what could possibly happen.

"*The greatest sources of our suffering are the lies we tell ourselves*, (Van der Kolk)."

What lies are you telling yourself? Are you believing the narrative that other people speak about you? Or, are you imagining the words that people are saying about you? Our experiences help to shape the perception of our reality. If we have experienced rejection, we expect to be rejected by everyone. God made each one of us with special gifts and abilities. Finding our purpose is something that some of us wrestle with. Sometimes we talk ourselves out of taking chances and being what God created us to be. We allow our trials and our trauma to imprison us in our minds.

Mental health is not something that is discussed regularly in the black community or within the church. For someone to acknowledge their mental problems that could be seen as a weakness. They could be labeled as crazy. Research has shown the challenges with discussing mental issues.

"In the Black community, there is often difficulty acknowledging psychological difficulties, but useful strategies including religious coping and methods such as pastoral guidance and prayer often are the most preferred coping mechanism." (Vance 2019)

The old church mothers would say, "just give it to God, and everything will be okay." I believe in the power of God and his ability to heal, but there has to be some discussions about trauma and mental illness. If we don't talk about it, it doesn't exist. That kind of thinking is flawed. We all experience trauma. Sometimes the trauma we experience leads to more problems. If we experience sickness or an injury to our bodies, we go to the doctor to find out what is wrong. That is not always true when dealing with psychological issues or problems. If we are willing to face those things that have impacted our lives, real growth and healing can happen.

I have spent a lot of time hiding my pain. That has made my life more difficult. There was a time when our family experienced five deaths over the course of two or three years. These losses severely impacted my life, but I wasn't ready to face the pain. My son's death was one of the most difficult things I've ever experienced. Robert was killed in a drive by shooting in 2008. He was 19 years old. Robert was not in a gang, he was in the wrong place at the wrong time. His death was traumatic for our family. I wrote about it in my book, Misery to Motivation. I didn't deal with the loss initially. I was so busy planning for the funeral and preparing for the trial of the person who killed him, that I suppressed my feelings. This was a mistake. I was hurting inside and it was eating me up. I hit a wall. I was ready to explode because everything around me didn't make any sense. I found a therapist and I began talking about the pain.

Releasing the Trauma

The trauma, hurt or disappointment I experienced impacts the way I look at life and how I approach situations. Whenever I experienced trauma, I interpreted as meaning that I wasn't wanted, I wasn't valued, I did not matter. When that happened, I developed ways to cope. Pain or suffering makes me hide. I run away and I hide. It seems safer. I had to realize that my pain did not disqualify me from operating in my purpose. My challenges and experiences prepared me for what's next. I cannot allow myself to remain stuck because of the unresolved pain.

The National Institutes of Health says, "Post Traumatic Stress Disorder (PTSD) is a disorder that develops in some people who have experienced a shocking, scary or dangerous event." Symptoms can include nightmares or unwanted memories, avoidance of situations that bring back memories, heightened reactions, anxiety or depression.

When I am stressed, I pray, I write in my journal or I exercise. Talking with a counselor or a therapist is a good way to process unresolved trauma. When I talked to my therapist it was good to hear my words and explore different ways to deal with the trauma. Stephanie Foo in her book *What My Bones Know: A Memoir of Healing From Complex Trauma* said, "Most of the world expects trauma and suffering. Most people live through it. It's not an exceptional, one time experience." The trauma we experience in our life sticks around. In the right setting and under the right circumstances we must face it. That is the only way we can completely heal and move past it.

Chapter Three

The Penultimate

> ***Except a corn of wheat fall into the ground and die, it abideth alone: but if it die, it bringeth forth much fruit" (John 12:24).***

God oftentimes uses natural things to explain spiritual concepts. These descriptions give believers the ability to see things from another perspective and through different lenses. The word penultimate is Latin in origin and it means, *occurring immediately before the last one: next to the last.* The concept or idea comes from athletics, namely the long jump in track and field. The long jump is comprised of three phases: the *approach*, the takeoff/ jump and the landing. The *penultimate step* in the long jump sequence is the step the athlete takes immediately before he jumps. This is the gathering step. During this phase, the jumper's center of gravity is lowered. The lowering prepares the body to go up. To execute a jump, many things have to work in concert to have success. Timing is everything.

Much like the long jump, life is filled with many ups and downs. The experience of the birth of child is one of the greatest feelings a person can experience. It represents a new beginning. This is a high moment. On the other hand, as our parents age and experience the transition from life to life eternal, dealing the death of a loved one can seem debilitating and difficult. This represents a down moment. Throughout our lives the phases of the long jump are played out over and over again. How we approach things in our lives contributes to our success.

At times it may feel like the down moments in our lives last so much longer than the ups. How we deal with adversity and difficulty determines how far we go and what we accomplish. The difficulty is found when things remain static or when no progress is being made. I've heard the Christian walk described as a race much like that of a marathon, but I have never heard it compared to the long jump event.

In 1968, Bob Beamon entered the Olympic Games in Mexico City as one of three long jumpers representing the United States. His best jump before these Olympic Games was 27 ft 2 in. He came into the Olympics as the odds-on favorite to win the gold medal.

Beamon warmed up like usual. It is his turn to jump. He runs down the runway expecting a good jump. He takes off in the air and lands a good distance out in the pit. He immediately looks back to see if he has fouled, but it was a clean jump. He now waits to hear the announcement of the distance. The announcer reads 8.91 meters (29 feet 2 1/2 inches). Upon hearing how far he jumped, he collapsed in disbelief. After setting the world record in the Olympics, Beamon never jumped as far. 26 feet 11 3/4 inches was his best jump after the Olympics.

Kairos

It was Bob Beamon's time to do something Great. The Kairos of God represents His divine timing. That is when everything lines up for greatness.

In this chapter, we will look at ***penultimate*** as a step in the process of change. Penultimate is the step you take before you jump or leap. You could be at that step: the place in your life where your struggle is turning around; your hopelessness turns to hope and the place where your midnight will turn to day.

Weeping may endure for a night, but joy comes in the morning. The penultimate leads us into our joyful morning.

Psalm 30:5 KJV

[5] ***"weeping may endure for a night, but joy cometh in the morning."***

This is the gathering step.

During the long jump, when the penultimate step is taken, the body goes down before it goes up. It is the bracing step or set up step. It is the set-up step that is preparing you for greatness. If this step is wrong; too long or too short, you won't jump as high, or as far. Your next step may not necessarily be your best step, but make sure it is purposeful. The penultimate is about getting into position before the leap...Your penultimate step is but a setup for you to launch.

We look at the negative things that happen in our lives as a punishment or even a curse. It could be interpreted negatively. We assume that we are cursed...God has forgotten about us....or that the anointing has left us. God has not forgotten you. You are exactly where he needs you to be right now.

Jeremiah 29:11

For I know the plans I have for you," declares the LORD, "plans to prosper you and not to harm you, plans to give you hope and a future.

One thing I'd like for you to remember while you are reading this book: time is relative to God. A day is as a thousand years. The timing between your penultimate step and your launch may go quickly or a longer period of time could pass between the phases. Don't get discouraged. God is still in control.

Waiting on God

Wait on God sounds so cliché. It sounds like something someone says when others are searching and finding no help. Waiting on God is more than a notion. It requires patience and a resolve that is unshakeable.

Woman with issue of blood (Mark 5:24-34 KJV)

> ***"25 And a certain woman, which had an issue of blood twelve years,***
>
> ***26 And had suffered many things of many physicians, and had spent all that she had, and was nothing bettered, but rather grew worse,***
>
> ***27 When she had heard of Jesus, came in the press behind, and touched his garment.***

28 For she said, If I may touch but his clothes, I shall be whole.

29 And straightway the fountain of her blood was dried up; and she felt in her body that she was healed of that plague.

30 And Jesus, immediately knowing in himself that virtue had gone out of him, turned him about in the press, and said, Who touched my clothes?

31 And his disciples said unto him, Thou seest the multitude thronging thee, and sayest thou, Who touched me?

32 And he looked round about to see her that had done this thing.

33 But the woman fearing and trembling, knowing what was done in her, came and fell down before him, and told him all the truth.

34 And he said unto her, Daughter, thy faith hath made thee whole; go in peace, and be whole of thy plague."

The woman with the issue of blood was isolated, ostracized, suffering, alone, and desperate. She suffered from this condition for 12 long years without relief. She spent all of her money going to doctor after doctor trying to find a cure. She reached a point in her life where she could not take any more. I'd imagine that she felt cursed, cut off or out. Per the law, a woman who was on her cycle or bleeding could not be around other people. Nothing and no one could heal her issue. This woman's struggle represents a phase in her life that is lacking and empty. She heard about Jesus and all of the wonderful things he had done. How he healed the sick and made the lame walk. She thought to herself, I must get near him. If he touches me or even lays his eyes on me I know my situation will change.

When she arrived at the place where Jesus was, there were so many people gathered around him hoping he would bless them. There was no way he was going to see her in this big crowd. She moved back and forth and tried to squeeze in to get close to Jesus, but it was not working. What do I have to lose, she thought. She gets on her knees and began to crawl through the crowd. At first, she couldn't get through, but she kept on pushing. People pushed her aside, but she kept pushing. They screamed at her, but she kept pushing. They talked about her but she kept pushing.

By the time she reached Jesus, she was running out of strength. She had rehearsed in her mind what she was going to say when she met him. As she tried to gather herself and stand up, she had no strength left. She reached out and tried to get his attention. All she could do was grab the hem or edge of his clothing. Immediately Jesus stopped and asked, who touched me? In that touch Jesus felt virtue leave him. He felt the woman's desperation. He felt her pain and suffering. Jesus felt her faith pulling on him.

V. 29 says immediately her bleeding stopped and she felt healed. This was a ***Kairos*** moment for this woman. Everything lined up perfectly for her to be healed, but she had to do something. We cannot wait for people to recognize our giftedness or need. It is important for us to do something and the first step in the process is humbling ourselves (down) and recognizing that God is in control. When HE inspires us to move, we have to move and do what HE instructs us to do.

As stated before, in order to go up and achieve greatness, one must go down. The step before the last step must be precise and specific. The woman made her next to last *(penultimate)* step purposeful. She lowered her center of gravity and went for it. Her life was changed forever. Before touching Jesus, she was disillusioned, disgusted, dissatisfied, disturbed and diseased. Many of us experience these emotions when things are not playing out in our lives like we think they should. Don't allow your desperation to mess up the blessing that God has coming your way. Don't settle.

Chapter Four

Overcoming Storms

I can see clearly now the rain is gone I can see all obstacles in my way

-Jimmy Cliff

I read a book almost 30 years ago by H. Beecher Hicks called, Preaching Through a Storm. He says something powerful in the book. He says, "everybody is either heading for a storm in the middle of a storm or coming out of a storm (Hicks)." He said storms are real for everybody. I know for a fact that storms have been real in my life. When I read the book almost 30 years ago, I was young and I had no idea what storms I could endure. Since that time, I've been through many storms. I spoke earlier about the period of time of two years almost three years where I lost a lot of people that were close to me. I lost my uncle, I lost another uncle, I lost my dad, lost my grandmother and then I lost my son. In the midst of all of this, it seemed like no matter what I did, people kept dying and it seemed like the storm was not ending.

There's a scripture that is two places in the bible; In the gospel according to Matthew (Matthew 8:23-27) and also in the book of Mark (Mark 4:35-41). It talks about Jesus calming the storm. He and his disciples were on the boat and they were sailing along. and Jesus is at the bottom of the boat and he is asleep. A storm comes upon the boat and the waves are overtaking the boat and they are assuming that they are going to perish in the midst of this storm. Some of the disciples said, "does he not care if we perish?" They wake him up he gets up speaks to the storm and the storm ceases.

Some of us are in that place right now where we're saying to ourselves does He not care if I perish? does he not care that I'm going through? I want you to know that he cares that you're going through and you're not going to perish. I know it seems like it right now, but you're not going to die.

You're going through and you can't see your way out because it might be cloudy or it might be raining it might be really bad out, but if you hold on just a little while longer, I know and I've experienced it, everything is going to be okay. Hold on just a little while longer because this too shall pass. This storm is going to pass and when this storm passes we're going to keep on moving.

I don't want you to get down on yourself and I don't want you to beat yourself up. You're might be asking yourself, what have I done wrong? Did I do this wrong or did I do that wrong? Some of the storms that we experience is about getting us to the next phase. We cannot get to the next phase until the boat reaches the other side. You're trying to get to the next phase you've been praying about it, saying, I need a promotion. I believe God that things are going to change in my life. Sometimes you have to go through some things to get to where you need to be.

The storms that you are experiencing, no matter how strong they are, no matter how tough they are, and no matter how it seems like you're not going to make it, they are preparing you for something greater. The storm is not permanent. God just like Jesus, was right there on that ship. He was with them during the storm and he's with you during the storm he's with me during this storm.

Last year, my daughter was sick and she was hospitalized for a week. We did not know what was going on so we were praying and believing that God was going to heal her. I'm grateful to say right now that she is healed.

Frustration

When I was a teenager, I purchased a bike from the PennyPower. I paid like 25 or 30 dollars for the bike. It worked perfectly when I first bought it, a few weeks later it broke. No matter what I did, I couldn't get the bike to work. Something was wrong with the chain, and the brakes. All kinds of different things were going wrong with the bike.

One day I decided to work on the bike so I sat on the front porch and proceeded to work on it. I worked for an hour, I worked for two hours and no matter what I did, I could not fix or resolve the problem. About two hours later, my dad came outside and he looked at me. He asked, Is everything okay?

I said yeah dad. I'm trying my best

To fix this bike and i just can't fix it

He said,

One thing you have to understand is you're frustrated and when you're frustrated, you can't think clearly. He said,

Walk away for a while. Go and do something else and come back to this later on.

I reluctantly walked away from the bike. I don't remember what I did, but I found something to do for an hour or so. I came back to work on the bike and within five minutes I fixed the problem.

What I didn't realize was my dad was watching me the entire time. He watched me be frustrated. He watched me try different things. He did not help me fix the bike. He could have done it himself. My dad was good at fixing things. He could have done something to help, but he watched me. He wanted me to figure it out for myself. He gave me some great advice and I use that same advice when I think about my life today.

There are some things in my life where I'm frustrated with how things are going. I am frustrated with how things are not working out and I think about my natural father's words, and then I think about my heavenly father, and the fact that he is sitting there watching. He's watching us now and he could step in he could turn the situation around and fix it. He's waiting for us to ask him for help. The advice from my father was, walk away for a moment come back and try it again when you're not frustrated.

Some of us are frustrated. You're in the middle of something and you're you've been struggling with it over and over and over again and you keep coming to the same result. You're not resolving the problem and God is saying to us that all we have to do is step away for a moment and put our trust in him. Proverbs 3 5 and 6 says trust in the lord with all your heart and lean not to your own understanding in all your ways acknowledge him and he will direct your path. That's just one scripture, but there's scripture after scripture after scripture where God reminds us to put our trust in him.

You may be carrying a weight. I know you are because I've been carrying weights around for a long time. I carry them on my shoulders because I feel like I have to be the one to solve the problems. God said allow him to give you advice allow him to show you how to solve the problem. Jesus says, "come unto me all ye who are weary and are heavy laden and I will give you rest." That was me, trying to fix that bike. I was weary, I was frustrated, and my natural father stepped in and gave me the advice that I needed in order to fix the problem. The same is true with your heavenly father, God wants to help you to fix your problem but, you have to allow him to do that. You must invite him in.

Chapter Five

God's Timing

When I was young, my little sister's godfather took us to an event around Christmas time. At this event there were many kids. The people hosting the event were giving away presents. I was thinking, wow, we're going to get a present. They gave each and every one of us a little raffle ticket. At the bottom of the raffle ticket, there was a number. Numbers were called over the loud speaker. We waited and waited and waited, and I kept looking at my number. As the numbers were called, kids would go up to the front and they would get a present. Some were small presents. Some were large presents. I don't know what they were, but I was waiting for my number to be called. The event was over and my number was not called.

We didn't leave empty handed. They gave us a little stocking with candy, so everyone received something. If your number was called, you got a bigger gift, you got a bigger present. As a little kid, that kind of stuck in my mind. Other people's numbers are being called? Whether it's your friends or your co-workers or other people that you know, you see great things happening for them.

And as you see great things happening for them, you are happy for them. Of course, you're excited for them. But even with the excitement, in the back of your mind, you're saying, what about me? Has God forgotten about me?

There's a story in the Bible where Jesus heals a man at the pool of Bethesda (John 5). At this place, there were different types of people who were sick. They were hoping for the moment to get healed. Once a year, an angel would come and trouble the water. As the water is troubled, the first person that stepped in the water would be changed, would be healed.

In this story, Jesus shows up at Bethesda and he walks past different people he walks up to this man and he asked the man a question. Jesus says, will you be made whole? And the man immediately says. Every time the water was troubled, or moved, somebody goes in in front of me, somebody beats me to the water. Jesus tells the man to take up his mat and walk.

How many of us feel that way sometimes? We feel like we've been beat out. we've been beat or someone else gets the reward. That's frustrating. It's frustrating because we're asking ourselves, when will it be my time? So, the man gives all of these excuses. He says this and that and everything like that. The man had been there for 38 years. Can you imagine being somewhere for 38 years? He is waiting for his time and he is waiting for his opportunity. He is waiting for his moment.

God knows who you are. He told Jeremiah, he said, Before I formed you in your mother's womb, I knew you.I know it's frustrating and I know it's tough. And in that frustration, we're watching other people bloom, bloom and prosper. We're still asking ourselves, when is it going to be my turn? Now, as Jesus shows up and talks to this man, he tells this man to take up your bed or take up your mat. And it says that the man picks up his mat. And he walks away. Many of us are waiting for our time. God knows our time.

During the time of waiting, it can be frustrating. We have to understand God's timing. God's timing is perfect. There are two different words in Greek for time. One of the words is Chronos, and that is like the time on a clock. There's another word for time, and that time is Kairos. This word for time means the opportune moment and it stands for God's timing, right? God's timing is very different than the clock time. And so even though he gives people visons, even though he told you about something that was going on, gave you a dream about what's going to happen in your life, in your family's life, it might not be time yet.

The Kairos moment has not come yet.

When that timing happened for the man at the pool of Bethesda, it was his time. The water was troubled by the angel and he missed out. Jesus is the water and he brings the water to him.

God will bring to you everything that he has for you. Another person cannot get your blessing. Somebody else cannot get your blessing. Sometimes it looks like that. You may have started at the same place as others, and it seems like other people are far ahead of you. We're saying, what about me? The question is, will we be ready when that moment happens? God is waiting. For this perfect time for you. In the book of Habakkuk, the bible says "the vision for the vision waits for the appointed time.

> ***For the revelation awaits an appointed time. It speaks of the end and will not prove false. Though it linger, wait for it, it will certainly come to pass.***
>
> ***(Habakkuk 2:3 NIV)***

God said it, it's going to happen.

God has given all of us a vision. He's given each and every one of us dreams. And those visions and those dreams were not given for no reason. They will come to pass.

But while we're waiting in our frustration, we find other things to do. In our frustration, we stop believing. I want to encourage you today to not give up, don't stop believing, because if you do, you will miss out on your Kairos moment. God has a way of doing things. Suddenly, suddenly, your moment will change. Suddenly you'll get a phone call. Suddenly somebody will recognize you. And you've been waiting and waiting for somebody to see you and see your gift. God is waiting for that moment. He will say now is the time. And when that happens, your life is will change.

We all need encouragement because there are times when people are right at the edge of giving up. They said, I've been believing this for a long time and people have talked me out of it. They said, why don't you try something else? Why don't you try another dream, try another goal, set another goal and try to achieve something else? Deep in your heart, deep in your soul, deep in your spirit you know what God has promised. God told you a long time ago, this is exactly what it is he has in store for you. When that suddenly moment happens, where everything is aligned, that's that Kairos moment. Everything lines up. Boom, boom, boom. And as it lines up, we see the fullness of what God has in store for you. Like that man that picked up his mat and walked. His life changed forever. For 38 years. He was lame for 38 years. He could not walk. Thirty-eight years. He was waiting for something to happen. Some of us have been waiting for ten years. five years, one year, 20 years, 30 years.

We've been waiting in and in the midst of our waiting, our frustration has been so strong that it hurts to believe. God said, if you hold on just a little while longer. Hold on just a little while longer, Hebrews 11:6 says, but without faith, it's impossible to please God. I want to please God and I want the things that I do to be pleasing in Him.

Timing is everything. Don't get frustrated and give up before your number is called. Waiting for my number to be called is frustrating. I understand waiting. I experienced that as a child and I've lived that life as an adult as well, but I've seen the goodness of God here in the land of the living. I've seen that goodness of God. I've seen him change things for my sake.

Please continue to believe. I want you to believe stronger than you've ever believed before. Go back and dust off that vision. Go back and look at it again, and as you look at it again, continue to speak it. Though it tarry, wait for it, it will not prove false. God knows where you are and he knows your timing.

Chapter Six

Get Ready

I was thinking about Joseph and the trials and the tribulations he experienced during his lifetime. I also thought about my own life and how easy it is to get discouraged when things look bad. It is easy to get discouraged when things just don't make sense.

In Genesis 50:20 it says,

> ***"as for you meant evil against me but god meant it for good in order to bring about this present result to preserve many people alive."***

Joseph was set apart. He was special.

He was his daddy's (Jacob) favorite son and it was shown. He had the coat of many colors so favor is all over him. It is easy to see and to understand that when favor is on your life what happens is, it not only brings light to you but it also brings darkness to you. In the midst of it bringing darkness, it is not fair. I have heard favor described as not being fair, but it brings types of attacks that many of us can't handle. In the story of Joseph, he tells his brothers about a dream he had. In the dream he sees himself rising up, but this was the spirit of God giving him the dream. His brothers said, we have to do something about this dreamer and they conspired to kill him, but then one of the brothers said no let's not kill him, let's sell him into slavery.

There are people who are conspiring against you because of the light that's on your life. You didn't ask for the light, but the light is the anointing. It chose you. When you're chosen by God he sets you apart and when he sets you apart, people begin to oppose the light because that light shows their own darkness. It exposes their own darkness. They feel inadequate.

Phrases they say are, look at him, he thinks he's all that, or look at her, she thinks she's cute she thinks she's this. Insecurities within other people brings out the jealousy. Joseph experienced what he experienced because of the insecurities within his brothers, but it was about God's plan. The scripture says, this was part of god's plan to get him where he needed to be. God is getting you where you need to be. Most of the time it is not an easy road to travel. When God is getting you where he needs us to be sometimes we go kicking and screaming.

Do you think Joseph would have said, I'm going over to Egypt? Joseph was comfortable. He was his daddy's favorite child. He was in a comfortable place. Sometimes God shifts our comfort zone to get us to where we need to be. He's making you uncomfortable to get you to where you need to be.

Joseph was sold into slavery by his brothers. He ends up at Potiphar's house and he goes through series of attacks and accusations. God was with him. Sometimes it feels like he's not present, but he's there. God says I will never leave you nor forsake you (Deut. 31:6). He's always there. He's going to be there even though it seems like he's not there. He was right there with Joseph in the pit. He was with Joseph at Potiphar's house. He was with Joseph when the woman falsely accused him of trying to rape her. He was with Joseph in the prison. God was with him when he interpreted the dreams. God was with him when he spoke to pharaoh and God placed him as second in command of the entire country. Joseph was in the perfect position when a famine hit the land. He was able to safe his entire family, even the ones who sold him in to slavery.

Your trial, your struggle, the things that you're going through in your life, God is preparing you for greatness. It doesn't feel like it right now because we're depressed. I called it. We don't always want to admit it. We're depressed, we're down, we feel like nobody gets us. In the midst of all of that, God is preparing you for greatness.

Isaiah 43 verse 2 says,

"when you pass through the waters, I will be with you and through the rivers they shall not overflow you when you walk through the fire you shall not be burned nor shall the flame scorch you it's God is saying right there the he's going to be with you along the way.

I have a question for you, can you trust God when things don't look like the promise? Can you trust God when people are lying on you? Can you trust God when everything doesn't make sense? Can you trust god when you can't see your way? It is like walking blind. Can you trust God?

We see this with Joseph. You cannot share your dreams with everyone. It's not that you're bragging or anything like that, you're just sharing what God has given you. You cannot share your dreams or visions with everyone. They may not have the capacity to handle the anointing that's on your life. They wouldn't know what to do with it. Some people are offended by your confidence, but God has given each and every one of us gifts. You have gifts, I have gifts but your gifts are different than my gifts and your talents are different than my talents. Each of us were given these to build the kingdom of God. It wasn't so that I could be better than you or you could be better than me. It was given so that we could build the kingdom of God.

Chapter Seven

Look at the Signs

My family traveled a lot when I was younger. My mom's family was from Oklahoma so we took frequent trips there. Most of the time, my uncle Sammy was the driver. He loved leaving the house early in the morning. We usually started our trip at three or four o'clock in the morning and we would arrive at the destination early.

One morning, everyone piled into the car and we were on our way. My brothers were asleep, but I was wide awake because I wanted to see everything. I was watching everything on the road. I saw a sign that read, DO NOT PASS. Something within me got really nervous because I was six years old, and I was learning how to read. My interpretation of the sign meant, don't pass this point because the road is getting ready to end. That's what I assumed. Uncle continued to drive and the DO NOT PASS sign came up again. I didn't know what anxiety was but I was anxious. I said oh no, it's coming up again so the road is getting ready to end.

.I had a limited understanding or a knowledge of what that sign meant. I didn't understand what it meant, but my uncle who was driving the car, knew exactly where he was going. He had been on that road many times. He knew the highways quite well. We'd travel on the backroads. He had his routine, his way of doing things. We all have our own routine. We have our way of doing things.

He was driving the car, it was his journey, I was just a passenger. Sometimes we are passengers on this journey of life. There will be fearful moments. During this trip I was afraid that the road was going to end, but the road was not ending. The Do Not Pass sign meant, this a was a no passing zone.

We arrived safely at our destination because he knew the road and he had traveled the route many times before. God knows your road. He knows where you are going and he knows what's coming up. He knows if there's a pothole, he knows if there is a roadblock or detour. God knows all of this, but we are not in tune with God.

I remember seeing bumper stickers that said, GOD IS MY CO-PILOT. There is an excitement about saying this. This is not true for me. God is my GPS and sometimes He allows me to drive. We have our own plans. We tell God our plans and we put it on the altar and we ask Him to bless the plan.

God told Jeremiah in 29:11,

> ***For I know the plans I have for you," declares the LORD, "plans to prosper you and not to harm you, plans to give you hope and a future.***

He knows what is coming. He's not like me afraid. I was scared because I was misinterpreting the sign.

Chapter Eight

Playing with Fire

I was an adventurous kid. Some would say I was a bad kid. I wouldn't say I was bad. I was raised to be obedient, to follow the rules and be respectful; to say yes sir and yes ma'am. A better description would be precocious. I watched and learned and grasped things. I was bored, so I found myself exploring. My dad was a smoker so I had access to cigarettes, lighters and matches. I was fascinated with fire. I was reckless. There is an old saying that says, if you play with fire, you will get burned.

One day I was playing with matches. As I was walking down the street. I lit a match and tossed it. The match flew into a yard and it hit a dry patch of grass. The grass caught on fire. It started to spread. I'm scared and I'm trying my best to put out the flame. I stomp and stomp. Eventually the flame is extinguished. I am looking around to see if anyone has seen what I had done.

I knew If my mom found out, I was in big trouble. Nobody saw me. Nothing was ever done. There remained a burn spot in the grass. That was the last time I played with fire.

Much like playing with fire that time, we play with fire in our lives. I learned a valuable lesson. In the 28th chapter of 1st Samuel King Saul is in a place where he could not hear from God. He seeks God and there is no response. The Philistine army is preparing to attack and he is afraid. The prophet Samuel had recently died so Saul had no one to talk to who could go to God on his behalf. Saul, in his desperation, put word out that he was looking for a woman with a familiar spirit. They find someone. He secretly goes to meet with the witch of Endor. Saul asks her to bring someone back from the dead. The lady says to him, who do you want to bring back?

Saul says, Samuel. The witch of Endor is fearful because Saul had banned all of the witches from practicing witchcraft. Saul makes a promise to her. He says, I will not punish you. The spirit of Samuel is brought back and Saul speaks to him. Samuel tells Saul the same thing he said when he was alive. He said, God has rejected you. He tells him that he and his sons will die in battle tomorrow and David will be the next king of Israel.

Saul was playing with fire. When we don't get the answer that we want, we find someone to give us an answer. Sometimes, we are looking for someone to agree with our perspective. We're looking for someone to agree with what is going on in our minds. That is not what God wants us to do. We should trust God wholeheartedly. When we are not trusting God, we seek out things that may tickle our fancy. We begin to play with fire. We may get a word or prophecy from the pastor of the church. We seek agreement by running to receive a word or a prophecy from another preacher somewhere else. If we cannot find someone with the confirmation or agreement that we are seeking, we may reach out to a psychic. This is dangerous. Please do not give random people access to your life. This may open a door and it may cause confusion in your life. It could also give the enemy permission to attack you, or set up a stronghold.

God has given us weapons to fight.

2 Corinthians 10:4-6 (The Amplified Bible) says, "The weapons of our warfare are not physical [weapons of flesh and blood]. Our weapons are divinely powerful for the destruction of fortresses. *We are* destroying sophisticated arguments and every exalted *and* proud thing that sets itself up against the [true] knowledge of God, and *we are* taking every thought *and* purpose captive to the obedience of Christ, being ready to punish every act of disobedience, when your own obedience [as a church] is complete."

Don't Give Up

When I was younger I could run and run and run and I didn't get tired. I could run all day. I had stamina. Let me try to run today, I run a little bit, stop, start walking. Run a little bit stop and start walking again. I can't run like I could when I was younger. I don't have the stamina. There's a scripture that talks about that. Isaiah 40 verse 30 and 31 it says, "*Even youths grow tired and weary and young men shall utterly fall but they that wait upon the lord shall renew their strength they should mount up with wings as eagles. They shall run and not grow weary, they shall walk and not faint.*"

It lets us know that if we put our trust, our hope in God, even in those moments of being tired and weary that if we wait on God, our strength will be renewed. He's going to renew our strength and then we'll run and not get tired right and we'll be able to walk and not be faint. God makes that promise to us there in Isaiah 40. There is a difference between just reading the word and actually living the word.

I want to encourage you today to wait a little while longer. I know some of us are on the verge of being ready to give up. We're right at the edge of being ready to quit. We want to give up because we've been trying the same thing over and over again and it has not worked.

One definition of insanity is doing the same thing over and over again and expecting different results. That's not always true because the word of God begins to tell us some other things. Galatians 6:7 says "be not deceived God is not mocked for whatsoever man so that shall he also reap." If you read down a little bit further in the 9th verse, it says and "be not weary doing good or be not weary in well-doing for in due season you shall reap if you faint not."

Don't give up. Don't give up. If you give up now, you might give up right before the blessing is revealed. Don't give up before your blessing is made manifest. Don't give up before the blessing comes into your life.

I heard the story years and years ago about the bamboo tree. The tree is planted in the ground and it's watered every single day but nothing happens. Nothing happens in the first month. Nothing happens in the first year or the second year or the third year, but they have to keep on nurturing it and watering it every single day. The first year, second year, third year, fourth year nothing happens. Between the fourth and fifth year, something begins to happen. Something begins to spring out of the earth. A blade and then within the next six weeks this bamboo tree grows to be 80 or 90 feet tall. People who see the tree blooming assume that it happened overnight, but it didn't happen overnight. Something was happening below ground. There was something happening beneath the ground that allowed it to grow and spring forth 80 to 90 feet in the air.

I don't want you to give up before the blessing comes your way because if the blessing springs up and somebody else comes along and grabs it. They walk into something where you have labored. Don't walk away from your blessing. You planted it, and watered it. Don't walk away from your blessing. You've nurtured it and now it's getting ready to spring forth. In this season, I need for you to be prepared to receive this blessing. You may feel like your dreams are being dashed, but if you wait a little while longer, you will reap.

Chapter Nine

Broken Chains

I pulled into a parking space on my job and I prepared for my day. As stepped out of my car, I saw something right next to where I was parked. It was an old, rusted chain. I didn't know where it came from, but I know that it was there for me to find. I picked up the chain, I put it in the trunk of my car and it just stayed there for about a week or so. And as I was praying, Spirit of God told me, that chain represents your freedom.

I'm said OK, God, what am I free from? You have been set you free from the chains that bind you, He said. I found out that most of the things that bind us are not external chains, but these chains that exist in our mind.

Internal chains. What is binding you? What are the things that keeps you in your box? What is keeping you in your place? What is keeping you from taking a chance, taking a risk?

When I was growing up, there was dogs all over the place. I have to admit, I am afraid of dogs. If I hear a dog, I'm paying attention and I'm always looking for an exit and I'm looking for a road. How do I how do I get out of here? My brothers and I knew where all the dogs were. We also knew which dogs would chase us. We jumped on top of cars to escape from dogs. We did all kinds of different things. One day I was walking through a neighborhood and I saw big dog, a great big dog. There was a thick chain attached to his collar and that chain was attached to a stake in the backyard. Whenever we would walk by, the dog would bark like crazy and run to the fence. The dog could only go so far based upon the parameters of how far the chain would allow it to go.

One day we're walking by and the dog did his normal routine. He's barking really, really loud. And as he's barking really, really loud, he comes to the edge of the fence. I look and I see that the stake that was normally in the ground was loose. The dog was free and not bound. He was free. It could have chased us. It could have done all kinds of different things, but it stopped at the edge of the fence. That was based upon the distance that the chain would allow him to travel. The dog had no idea it was free.

How many of us are like the dog? We are free, and we've allowed our old mindset, our old ideas or even what other people think of us, to keep us in our place. We started running. As I think back about it, that dog could have hurt us. What about you? What could you be doing right now? Now the chain is broken. And now that the chain is broken and you're not bound by the chain any longer, what is stopping you from being the best you that you can be? What is stopping you from achieving the things that you want to achieve?

Galatians 5:1 (New Living Translation) says, "So Christ has truly set us free. Now make sure that you stay free, and don't get tied up again in slavery to the law." Jesus has set us free from many different things. He gave his life for us so that we could be free.

What is stopping you? Is it a mindset? Is it an idea? Is it fear? Or thoughts that other people have of you? What are you doing? The chains are broken, like that dog, we are thinking that it is still bound.

In Plato's Allegory of the Cave, he talks about some men who are chained together inside of a cave. They've been chained there since they were young. All they can see behind them is what appears to be light. And that light reflects certain images. They appear as shadows on the wall. They are chained, their motion is limited, and all they can see is the shadows that are on the wall.

And as they're looking at these shadows on the wall, these men who are chained together, have an idea of what these shadows are. That's that. I know that's a man. I know. That's a woman. That's a dog. I know. That's this. They're seeing all of these different things. One day it says that one of the guys gets free and he breaks free of his chain. He finds his way out and he goes toward the light. As he goes toward the light, he walks outside of the cave. He can't see too well because all he'd seen was darkness and all he'd seen was shadows that were on a wall. He's tries to get his bearings. He's begins to see things that may not look exactly like what was on that wall. This is reality and this is real.

As he is looking at things, he sees himself and he sees a tree or he sees a man, and he realizes something, the things that he thought he saw based upon the shadows on that on that wall, they were different. He goes back into the cave. He begins telling the people inside the cave about what he saw outside of the cave. He's telling them about what is happening outside. They don't believe him. He says, come on, let me get you out of here. I want to get you out of here. And I want you to see for yourself that the things that we see on the on the wall, is not real. I want to show you the reality. The did not want to leave the cave.

Some of us would rather be bound to our current condition instead of experiencing the unknown. The unknown is scary. It is scary because we don't know what's going to happen. We're comfortable in our current state even being bound and we have the opportunity to be free.

Jesus came and he set us free from many things. To achieve and experience that freedom, we have to accept the fact that we've been set free. And then we have to do is open our mind to a new way of thinking, a new paradigm. And this new way of thinking will contradict what we've known our entire lifetime. And, yeah, that's tough. That's tough. It's difficult. It's difficult because it means that I have to give up what I thought and then I have to be open to see what's new, what is possible.

I want to challenge you because you've been set free. You can go back to that place like the dog or like the men in the cave. You can go back to that place where you're saying, I'm going to stay right here bound by what the chain would allow me to do. Or you can open yourself up to seeing greater things.

What's in store for you? "Eye has not seen, nor ear heard, Nor have entered into the heart of man The things which God has prepared for those who love Him" (1 Corinthians 2:9)

So, God is preparing something for us. He's preparing some stuff for everyone. He prepared them even before we were born. One of things that he prepared for you is greatness. But this greatness is hard to imagine in your current state because all you see is the chain. I want to tell you right now; the chain is broken.

Your chain, the thing that's holding you back has been broken. That excuse is gone. What are you going to do about it? What are you going to do differently now? There has to be a mind shift. My mind has to shift from where it's been and open up to something brand new, and this brand new may be uncomfortable.

This is new for me, but I'm not bound.

> ***You, dear children, are from God and have overcome them, because the one who is in you is greater than the one who is in the world. 1John 4:4***

There are some things inside of you that you don't even realize and you can't experience them because you're stuck connected to whatever you're bound to. I want us to live free. I want us to live with true liberty.

Think about the things that you want to do, but you are unable to do them because there are barriers in your way. I want you to write the things down on your paper. And these are the barriers that keep me from doing these things. In one column I want you to write some of your dreams. In the next column write barriers. That's what I want you to do. You have the column of your wants/dreams, and you have the column of barriers. As you're looking at the column of wants or dreams and the column of barriers, the barriers are your chains. They are the chains that are keeping you from experiencing greatness. These chains are keeping you stuck in that place.

I want you to begin to dream past your chains. What would you do if all of a sudden all of your barriers were gone?

Take your piece of paper with all of your words and give this to God. There is power in prayer. James 5:16 says "Confess your faults one to another, and pray for another, that you may be healed. The effectual fervent prayer of a righteous man availeth much." Effectual fervent in the Greek is energeo. It means *to be operative, to be at work.*

What would I do? What would I do? As these things are written down, we look more at the barriers, than we look at the dreams. Stop focusing on your barriers because your barriers have more life. Your barriers have more life than your dream. You're giving more life to the barrier than you are to your dream. You worship your chain and you focus on that more than your dream.

I want you to dream a dream like never before. How do I begin to do these things? I want you to try something new. Try something new. Try something that you've been afraid to try. I want you to try it. You have your dreams on the left side. You have your barriers on the right side. Stop thinking about those barriers. Choose one of those dreams that you have on there. Set a goal toward achieving one of those dreams.

Say, for instance, you want to be this. I've always wanted to do this in my life. Find a way to learn more about it and see what you can begin to do. That's what I want you to do. And so that's what God wants us to do. He wants us to live. He wants us to live in a way where he's glorified in our lives. God is glorified when we are doing the things that he created you to do. That's a beautiful thing and that is wonderful. I don't want to be like that dog that's chained in that yard and I don't want to be like those men that were chained inside of that cave. I want to live the life that God has set for me to live.

Chapter Ten

Change

"Being confident of this very thing, that he which hath begun a good work in you will perform it until the day of Jesus Christ:"

Philippians 1:6

God has a plan for all of us. All of our plans are different. He knew what we would do even before we were born. A baby comes into the world with DNA from their mother and their father. Some people may say that a new born baby looks just like their mother or their father. Who they are is yet to be seen. Only time will reveal who they are. As time passes they learn. They learn how to use their limbs, how to crawl, how to walk, how to talk. They change along the way. As the baby grows into adulthood change is happening. If you look at my baby picture and a picture of me now you'd say how did that little baby become this man. A lady at the hospital told my mom after I was born that she might not want the baby picture from the hospital. I guess I was not much of looker. The only way to explain it is God. God is so amazing. He creates and fulfills.

We experience changes. Change occurs constantly. Some of us are fighting change. We are trying to hold on to what we were in the past, what we had. Others are excited about change and they want to change. We all experience change in our lives. When I was growing up, I had a tremendous growth spurt. I was about 15 years old. I remember some painful nights. I would be in so much pain, I could feel pain in my knees. I felt my body stretching. My body was stretching and I didn't know what was going on. Some nights, I'd be in tears because, the pain, was intense. I was stretching from one size to another. I was growing out of my clothes, my voice was changing, everything about, me, was changing. In the midst of the discomfort, I did not know what to do. I grew five or six inches in a year. This change was unlike anything I'd experienced.

I made it through the discomfort. It was challenging, but I made it. Over the next few years I continued to grow. When the pain showed up, I knew what was happening. As a teenager I grew 10 inches. I went from being average height to being a tall person. With those changes I had to make some adjustments.

Spiritual change

My first year of college I was all by myself in a different town. I was finding my way. I was going to school and playing basketball. I chose this particular college because I wanted to play basketball and it had a good law school. I wanted to become a corporate attorney. I was young and I really didn't fit in. I'm not saying that I was perfect. I was a young boy coming of age and finding my way away from home. I attended church as often as I could because I felt like that was the right thing to do.

I remember when a change was taking place on the inside of me. I had a friend back home named Charles, who shared the gospel with me. He said God is real and Jesus died for all of us. All you have to do is pray and ask for Him to come into your heart. I was being transformed. One night I was in my apartment listening to a song by Walter Hawkins called Changed. I listened to the song over and over again. Tramaine Hawkins leads this song and she says,

"A wonderful change has come over me

A wonderful change has come

Over me

Yes he changed

My life complete

And now I sit

I sit at my savior's feet ." (Walter Hawkins, 1975)

This night I got on my knees and I prayed. I said, God I believe that Jesus died for me and I want you to come into my heart. I felt the change and my life has not been the same. Anytime I hear that song I immediately go back to the moment when my life changed. It makes me feel good.

The process of change

Although changed happened to me in my heart, it was still a process that I had to go through. I had to grow up and learn more about God. How did he see me? What did He want me to be or to do? I felt different, but where did I fit? Where did I belong? After many changes, ups and downs, I committed my life to preaching and teaching.

Job 14:14 says,

If a man dies shall he live again? All the days of my appointed time will I wait until my change is come.

Why do we fight against change. Is it a sense of control? We want things to remain the same, but in order for God to get the glory…there has to be change. We can look at nature and watch the change process in action…

The butterfly

The butterfly experiences a process that is different than humans. Butterflies lay eggs and these eggs enter a larvae stage and produces a caterpillar. The caterpillar is not an adult. It eats and prepares for the next phase. It does not reproduce.

The process of a caterpillar becoming a butterfly is an arduous one. The caterpillar knows inherently that change is on the horizon. They begin to eat certain foods to sustain them during their transformation. They separate themselves so that the process can take its' course. Isolation.

As we are being transformed and changed…we have to separate ourselves from certain people because they will not allow change to take place in our lives. They will always remember when you used to do that…or say that….or be thus and so.

Isolation is a lonely process.

The caterpillar builds his house or chrysalis to protect itself and keep it safe during the transformation. He builds this out of the mucus in his mouth. The caterpillar goes through a change while it is inside of the chrysalis pouch.

When the time comes and the caterpillar has transformed into a butterfly, the butterfly breaks free from the pouch. This is a new creature, a new being. Change has occurred.

The butterfly gains strength by breaking out of the pouch. Its wings are strengthened and it gets stronger. Once it breaks through a new life begins. It is no longer a caterpillar. A butterfly emerges and it prepares to fly.

God has great things in store for your life. Do not fight the process of change?

Chapter Eleven

Play to Win

A few years back I was playing in a pickup game and a young man was guarding me. And the young kid is holding me and I turned around and I shoot the ball. The ball goes up. I miss the shot. I get a rebound. I love playing basketball. At least I used to enjoy playing basketball. It was a way to relieve stress exercise and clear my mind. During this particular game, the kid stops me and he asked a question. He said, what are you doing? I said, what do you mean? I said. I'm playing basketball? He said it again, what are you doing? You're just throwing the ball up there. You just throwing the ball up there. You have no intention of making it. I say, man, no, I'm trying to make it. He said, no, you are not. You're not trying to make it.

We continued playing. After the game was over, I went my way and he went his way. I've never seen him again. I realized something. The kid was right. I was out there exercising. I was just playing. I was not playing to win. I was playing to play. And as I thought about that, I thought about how I've lived my life. Instead of playing to win, I've played to play, I'm just happy to be there, happy to be on the court, happy to be on the job, happy to be doing this or that and not really trying to win. I am happy to belong. When we begin to play, just to play, or exist just to exist, we are not doing what God created us to do. God created you to shine. He created you to be the very best you that you can be.

I challenge you to be the best version of yourself. What does that look like? Some of us have been just playing to play, just existing, just living a life for a long time. And in doing that, what has happened is, is that we assume that is our normal. We've created that to be our normal. But that's not what God wanted it to be.

God didn't intend for that to be normal. God intended you to experience great things, but certain things may have happened in your life. Trauma may have happened in your life. You may have lost someone you love. You may have had a heart break. Something may have happened in your life that has caused you to say, I'm not going to give it my all anymore. When I give it my all, I lose, or I might fail. That's not trusting God and that's not operating by faith. I quit dreaming a long time ago. A lot of us quit dreaming a long time ago because we settled into that place of just existing. We're not fulfilling the life that was created for us to live.

I want to live the life that God has created for me to live. God has plans for me and he has plans for you. Those plans are not dependent upon how good you are. And I say this all the time. We look at our lives and we say, well, I've done this, I've done this and I've done all of these things. and this disqualifies me. No, God sent his son Jesus to die on the cross for you and for me. And he raised him from the dead so that we will be in good standing and right standing with God.

I want you to know that God sees you as complete, not incomplete. He sees you as whole. He sees you as brilliant and whatever that plan may be, it's between you and God. Stop playing it safe, you're not helping anybody. Stop playing it safe. Now, see, I don't want to get to the end of my life and be thinking about the things that I could have done.

In 1955, at the age of 36 the late great Jackie Robinson stole home base in game 1 of the World Series. Many would say that he was past his prime to try such a feat, but Jackie Robinson wasn't concerned about his age or anything else. His focus was on scoring, and winning the game. The Brooklyn Dodgers were playing the New York Yankees, and were down 2 runs in the top of the 8th inning. What did he have to lose? He had everything to gain. The pitcher, Whitey Ford, pitched the ball and Jackie takes off running for home plate. Waiting at the plate was one of the greatest catchers ever to play the game, Yogi Berra. Jackie slides into home and the umpire yells, SAFE. Even though the Dodgers lost the game, they won the World Series. Jackie Robinson played to win.

What risks are you willing to take? Playing it safe will keep you in your current place. If you want to go to new heights and explore the greatness within, you are going to have to take a risk and be focused on a goal. Don't allow your age, your position, your history or your circumstances to keep you from taking a risk and becoming your best. God created you to shine. Not because you are better than everyone else, but because he wants us all to be our very best, and when we shine…He is glorified. Play to Win! He didn't design you or create you to be average.

The Underdog

In 1st Samuel 17, young David was asked by his father to take provisions to his three older brothers. They were fighting for King Saul against the Philistines. When David arrived, he saw a giant mocking the Israelites. Goliath dared anyone to oppose him. The Israelites were hiding. David didn't understand. His brothers teased him and asked him what he was doing there. Who is taking care of the sheep, one of them asked. David spoke what was on his mind. Word got back to King Saul and he sent for David.

David told King Saul, "your servant will go and fight him". Saul said, "you are a young man, and he has been a warrior from his youth." David goes on to tell him how he had killed a lion and a bear when they attacked his sheep. He said, "the lord who rescued me from the paw of the lion and the paw of the bear will rescue me from the hand of this Philistine." King Saul said, "Go and the Lord be with you." He fits David with armor. David said, "I cannot go in these, because I am not used to them." He chose five smooth stones from the brook. With his sling in his hand he went to fight Goliath.

When Goliath saw David, he saw a young handsome little boy standing up to fight against him. He said, "come here, and I will give your flesh to the birds." David said, "you come against me with the sword, spear and javelin, but I come against you in the name of the Lord Almighty, the God of the armies of Israel, whom you have defied." He goes on to tell him, that he will defeat him.

Goliath moved closer to fight. David ran as fast as he could to fight. He reached in his bag and pulled out a stone. He slung it, the stone hit Goliath in the forehead, and he fell to the ground. David defeated Goliath with a stone. After he was defeated, the Philistine army fled. David was seen as the underdog. He was operating with God on his side. He attacked Goliath with the Lord Almighty with him. From this moment on, David's life changed.

David played to win. We play to win by having God on our side. There is no reason to hide from the enemy or anything that opposes us. Romans 8:31 says, "If God is for us, who can be against us." David looked like the underdog, but he was in a powerful position because God on his side.

The average level of existence that you have experienced is not what he created for you. It is a safe place for you, safe. You've created this safe place. Saying, I'm OK. I'm good. But it's not great. It's not brilliant, and it's not to the capacity that God has in store for you. Stop playing it safe. Stop playing to play and start playing to win. I am determined that I will play to win.

Epilogue

I got off track. I lost myself a long time ago. I've been on a journey to find me. While on the road to find myself, I learned a few things that has helped. I learned that I cannot do this all alone. I need God. I learned to put on my own mask first. That means I have to release the things that I have been carrying and I have to take care of myself. I ***unpacked*** my bag and I started to address my trauma. I realized that the low areas in my life were preparing me for something greater. It doesn't matter how many storms I encounter, I'm not here by myself. It may not look like it, but God's timing is perfect. There are triggers that affect me and anxiety appears based upon my misinterpretation of signs. Trying to cope while playing with fire leads to more trouble.

I'm free - My chains are broken. I've been set free. I am special to God. I am fearfully and wonderfully made. There is a line in Kipling's poem IF, *"If you can meet with triumph and disaster and treat those two impostors just the same"*. In life we will experience some good times and some bad times, but God made each of us unique. There is no one else like you. Don't allow your success or your failure to define you. We are not defined by what we do. God created us to shine. Don't allow the past or your current situation to keep you from trying to be your very best. To be the best version of myself, I must play to win. I am not competing with anyone else, I am working on being the best version of myself.

References

The American Pyschological Association

Brown, B. (2017). Braving the Wilderness. Vermilion.

Elliott, R. K. (1967). "Socrates and Plato's Cave". *Kant-Studien*. **58** (2): 138.

Foo, Stephanie (2022). *What My Bones Know: A Memoir of Healing from Complex Trauma. Random House*

Hicks, H. B. (1987). *Preaching Through a Storm*

Harris, R. (2012). *Misery to Motivation.*

Kipling, R. (1954). *Rudyard Kipling's verse: Definitive edition*. London: Houghton and Stoughton

Merriam-Webster.com Dictionary, Merriam-Webster, https://www.merriam-webster.com/dictionary/addicted

https://www.merriam-webster.com/dictionary/average

Plato, Republic Allegory of the Cave Book VII *The Republic*

U.S. Department of Health and Human Services, National Institutes of Health, National Institute of Mental Health. (Updated 2019) Post Traumatic Stress Disorder Retrieved from https://www.nimh.nih.gov/health/topics/post-traumatic-stress-disorder-ptsd

van der Kolk, B. A. (2014). *The Body Keeps Score: Brain, Mind and Body in the Healing of Trauma.* Viking.

Van Peebles, M. (1991). New Jack City. Warner Bros.

New International Version Bible. (2011). The NIV Bible. https://www.thenivbible.com (Original work published 1978)

King James Bible. (2017). King James Bible Online. https://www.kingjamesbibleonline.org/ (Original work published 1769)

Vance, T, A PhD (2019). Columbia University Department of Psychiatry, News

(Ed.), *Addressing Mental Health in the Black Community*

The amplified Bible: Containing the amplified Old Testament and the amplified New Testament. (1965). Grand Rapids, Mich: Zondervan Pub. House.

(2004). Holy Bible: New Living Translation. Wheaton, Ill: Tyndale House Publishers.

About The Author

Riccardo L. Harris, a native of Wichita, KS., A former public-school educator and coach, Riccardo is a staunch advocate for urban youth, promoting education and character building as an alternative to the senseless violence that plagues many urban communities. The recipient of various community awards and recognitions, Riccardo strives to impact urban communities and to help youth avoid becoming victims and perpetrators of violence. In addition to his work with youth, Riccardo is also a published author, noted public speaker and a pastor at Resurrection Community Church, where he has served for 27 years. Riccardo and his wife Rosaland have been married for 30 years, they have three children and five grandchildren.

Connect with Riccardo Harris

Riccardo Harris
@riccopastor

Resurrection Community Church
944 S. Topeka
Wichita, KS 67211

website: www.riccardoharris.com

Woodstock....a moon landing.

A scholar

Preacher ...to some

Teacher of many

Husband...father..Grandfather ...love my family

Dreamer...thinker...make the world better.

Half full.....

Trust is given....respect is earned

A giver...who expects nothing in return

Overcomer......

Respectful....responsible....resilient

Battles lost...but victories won.

Will not be defined....by anyone.

Learner...researcher...observer

Publisher....writer...producer

Love hard...but forgive as well

This is my story...it is mine to tell

The color of my skin....my hue....hated and reviled

Underestimated...misunderstood....I'm invisible

Layers are many

Some just look at my face

They don't really see me..they don't know my place

Entertainer

Musician

Athlete

Smile...laugh....play the game

Courageous conversations have helped me to grow

I never...ever....share...all that I know

I have much to learn....and much to give

Faith

Hope

Love

So....

From faith to faith and glory to glory

I will succeed......this is my story